ALIAS IRENE

Elisabeth Murawski

Fernwood
PRESS

Alias Irene
©2026 by Elisabeth Murawski

Fernwood Press
Newberg, Oregon
www.fernwoodpress.com

All rights reserved. No part may be reproduced
for any commercial purpose by any method without
permission in writing from the copyright holder.

Printed in the United States of America

Cover and page design: Mareesa Fawver Moss
Cover image: *Study for Improvisation V* by Vassily Kandinsky
   on exhibit in the Minneapolis Institute of Art
Author photo: James O'Gara

ISBN 978-1-59498-192-0

Elisabeth Murawski's *Alias Irene* is another high point in this renowned poet's writing life. With exceptional vision, she transforms family, history, art, and literature into lanterns that light the world in ways never seen before. One poem ends, "Her heart wanting the world to be enough." This is significant because precise and elegant language make this world more than enough for poetry readers, Murawski's beneficiaries.

—GRACE CAVALIERI
Maryland Poet Laureate 2018-2023

With a "heart that knows its way in the dark," Elisabeth Murawski offers us these taut poems fraught with grief. Hers is a landscape of uncertainty where the sky is "cruel, tossing back / my black balloons, / pulling from its sleeve / rabbits of cloud." Startling imagery and a sense of our shared mortality run through these moving pages, with "purple crocuses / surviv[ing] late snow / to die." Faith is the "invisible thread" holding her world together, but just barely: "I break the arms off the crucifix. / I wrap those arms around me / as far as they will go."

—NANCY NAOMI CARLSON
author of *Piano in the Dark*

Land, love, and loss lend images and inspiration to Elisabeth Murawski in *Alias Irene*; she curates scenes and questions strewn from the immediately personal and familial to the sympathetically imaginative, and the result is a moving collection that asks readers to be present in the poems, to sit with the questions they ask, and to "chew on [Murawski's] words / with sensitive teeth" (from "On Reading a Chinese Poet"). The collection flows seamlessly within and between its four parts, and I found it difficult to put down, curious as to what sort of poem came next, drawn in.

—JULIAN KANAGY

editor-in-chief of *The Wild Umbrella*

Elisabeth Murawski's sculpted poems are one part Emily Dickinson, one part Anne Carson (*Eros the Bittersweet*), fully alive with ghosts, grief, and grace, not unlike Max Porter's novel, *Grief Is the Thing With Feathers*. Gothic threads become switchbacks between faith and requiem. Love is a juggling act played out from Hiroshima to the Sangre de Cristo mountains. She understands life is about giving and taking away. But how does one keep grief at bay? Or death? Or time? Murawski's answer is to open the gate and allow the blessings to fall like rain.

—RICHARD PEABODY
editor of *Gargoyle Magazine*

*To angels who show up,
ordinary as olive trees in Gaza,
sunflowers in Ukraine.*

TABLE OF CONTENTS

Acknowledgments 11
I 15
   A Declaration 16
   The Dollmaker's Daughter 18
   Child Wearing a Red Scarf 20
   Only the Sky 21
   Afternoon at Fort Washington 24
   At the Frost Place, August 1984 25
   The Arrival of Grace 26
   Suor Anna 28
   Teresa's Last Foundation 30
II 31
   Madeline Is Melancholy 32
   Alias Irene 33
   Bide a Wee 34
   Old Woman's Pivot Story 36
   Daughter with Camera 37
   Blessings and Curses 38
   Time Piece 40
   Law 41

The Letter 42
Troubled by an Angel 44
School Physical 46
Bride Doll 48
Ignominy on Garland Avenue 50
Petition to a Grandmother 52
Mother and Daughter 53
Sutra 54
Committed Here 56

III 57
A Room Like This 58
Between a Bullet and Its Target 59
Against the Wind 60
In a Russian Vein 61
Lineage 62
Shipwreck 63
Sunday in Vermont 64
Snakes at Fort Washington 65
To Your Good Address 66
Buttons 67
The Audience 68
The Rehearsal 69
Dark Circle 70
Historic Marker 71
Brief 72
The Confession 73
On Reading a Chinese Poet 74
I smile at you 75
As the Crow Flies 76

IV 77
Prologue 78
She looks everywhere 79
H.D. Yearning for D.H. 81
On a Seventh-Century Couple
   of Painted Clay 82

Emma Hardy Speaks from the Grave 84
Saying the Unsaid 85
Choices 86
Elegy for Green Eyes 87
With No Thoughts of Loneliness 88
The Fault, Dear Brutus 90
March 92
Memorial Photo—Spoleto Cemetery 93
Shenandoah 94
as I grow old 95
Epistle 96
Title Index 97
First Line Index 101

ACKNOWLEDGMENTS

Thanks to the editors of the journals who have published individual poems that appear in these pages and to Eric Muhr for giving *Alias Irene* a home at Fernwood Press. I am grateful to my teachers, Linda Pastan, C.K. Williams, and Peter Klappert, and to loyal friends who have supported and encouraged my work, especially Walter Cummins, Jeanne Sorrentino, Sue Lawless, Grace Cavalieri, David Kuebrich, Betsy Beyler, Nita Congress, Rick Peabody, Sue Hoffmeyer, Nancy Naomi Carlsen, Elisavietta Ritchie, Saideh Pakravan, Barri Armitage, Rebecca Foust, Elizabeth Stoessl, Sharon Ewing, and Susan Bianconi.

ALASKA QUARTERLY REVIEW .... Against the Wind
ALEMBIC .... The Letter;
Madeline is Melancholy;
Memorial Photo—Spoleto Cemetery
ALKALI FLATS .... With No Thoughts of Loneliness
ANTIETAM REVIEW .... Snakes at Fort Washington;
Buttons;
Daughter with Camera

ARTEMIS	Troubled by an Angel
ARTS AND LETTERS	Teresa's Last Foundation
THE BIRMINGHAM REVIEW	Shenandoah; Saying the Unsaid
THE BRIDGE	Old Woman's Pivot Story; Time Piece
COMMONWEAL	Law
CRAZYHORSE	Bide-A-Wee; Blessings and Curses
CUMBERLAND POETRY REVIEW	Arrival of Grace
DOUBLETAKE	School Physical
ELLIPSIS	The Fault, Dear Brutus
FIELD	Sutra
FINE MADNESS	As the Crow Flies; March
FOLIO	Prologue
GARGOYLE	Elegy for Green Eyes; I smile at you
HAYDEN'S FERRY REVIEW	Epistle
I-70 REVIEW	Sunday in Vermont
ILLUMINATIONS	Petition to a Grandmother
THE JOURNAL	Lineage; In a Russian Vein
THE LITERARY REVIEW	Mother and Daughter; On Reading a Chinese Poet
MANY MOUNTAINS MOVING	The Confession
OHIO REVIEW	A Room Like This
ONTARIO REVIEW	Bride Doll
POET LORE	Brief; To Your Good Address; The Rehearsal; Between a Bullet and Its Target; Afternoon at Fort Washington

POETRY NORTHWEST .... A Declaration;
                              Committed Here;
              On a Seventh-Century Couple of Painted Clay
PUERTO DEL SOL .... Historic Marker;
                          Child Wearing a Red Scarf;
                                       Suor Anna;
                              H.D. Yearning for D.H.
SHENANDOAH .... Emma Hardy Speaks from the Grave
SOUTH CAROLINA REVIEW .... Dark Circle;
                                       Shipwreck
TAR RIVER POETRY .... Choices
VIRGINIA QUARTERLY REVIEW .... As I Grow Old;
                                    Only the Sky
WEST BRANCH .... Alias Irene
THE WIDENER REVIEW .... The Dollmaker's Daughter
WILLOW SPRINGS .... The Audience;
                              She Looks Everywhere;
                          Ignominy on Garland Avenue
WORDWRIGHTS .... At the Frost Place, August, 1984

    The following poems also appeared in the chapbook, *Troubled by an Angel*: "The Arrival of Grace," "Troubled by an Angel," and "On a Seventh-Century Couple of Painted Clay."

    "Emma Hardy Speaks from the Grave" won the 2011 Graybeal-Gowen Poetry Prize (*Shenandoah*).

    "Teresa's Last Foundation" appeared on Poetry Daily, April 2013.

I

What shall I do with the body I've been given,
So much at one with me, so much my own?
—Osip Mandelstam, *Stone*

A Declaration

I am no chip of broken pottery.
I am no blue and white petroglyph
on a canyon wall.
I am no eye of turquoise.
I am no lavender door, no lavender
window jamb.
I am no kachina with hair
the color of dried blood.
I am no comb with teeth full of sand.
I am no mountain stream scrubbing
stones.
I am no bridge made of rope.
I am no snowy peak telling you
to change your life.
I am no moonstone suggesting possibilities
wild as deer.
I am no bear looking up surprised,
sniffing the air.
I am no iron pyrite warming your hand.
I am no straw sombrero tossed
on a chair.
I am no hoodoo built of red rock.
I am no cottonwood leaf blown down,
no Russian olive leaf.
I am no guitar, no flute
lonely in a major key.
I am no tequila laced with salt.
I am no scorpion in your shoe,
no rattler right behind
your reaching hand.
I am no current, no cross winds.
I am no beauty, no strength.
I am no sky-blue shock to the heart.

I am no mind, no soft belly.
I am no heaven, no earth.
I am no answer.
I am no answer.

The Dollmaker's Daughter

I just got tired of it,
that bee-stung kewpie smile
through every flood
and hurricane.

There was no blood in her.
Her fingers
could never be pricked
and touched to mine

to make us one.
She'd just lie there, eyes
closed, waiting for life
to be over. Or sit up

straight as I posed her
but hardly awake.
I could only take
so much of my own imagination

feeding her lines,
making up
her teacup history.
I began

by smashing in her face.
Now she looked the same
as any abused child.
I debated

between a knife
and a fortuitous fall.
The stairs won.
I stood at the top

looking down where she lay
as if she'd jumped,
the soft body mute,
the broken arms and legs

with archless feet,
so many pieces in flat pink
the color of Italy
in my geography book.

Child Wearing a Red Scarf

Vuillard painted them
as if he stood
directly behind on the curb,
banding her hair
with a scrap of blue,
cutting off the man
at the shoulders
as they pursue
the moment he pursues.
They are about to cross
the boulevard.

The child aims her body
straight ahead
toward a cluster of women
in black gowns,
some of which are daubed
with the same red
as her scarf
and the print of her dress.

This causes one's eye
to move from the child
to the women
and back again
as if in conversation.

So that one barely
notices, at first,
how the man's grip
on the girl's hand
is too tight, almost fierce
to protect or possess,
as she lifts
one tiny black shoe.

Only the Sky

> *There came a cloud*
> *and overshadowed them*
> *and they feared as they*
> *entered into the cloud.*
>   —Luke 9:34

1

It was early. Many
were barefoot. Some
stole clogs from doorsteps
and bolted, as if
staying in motion
could keep them alive
at ground zero.

Hiroshima blistered
at sea level.
It was the Catholic feast
of Jesus glorified
on Mt. Tabor.

Luke writes
the light about Jesus
was so great his raiment
turned white
and glistering.

The apostles
to behold this
transfiguration

must have
shielded their eyes.

2

Tanaka Kiyoku
fleeing the city on fire
saw "a giant tree burning
from its middle."

Did she know the hard
inner pith of a tree
is called heartwood?

There is no heartwood
in the family of trees
called ficus religiosa,
or bodhi,

beneath which Buddha sat
to be the light.
It is said these trees,
having no heartwood,

are truly empty.

3

In "A Child Remembers,"*
Tanaka Kiyoku, maybe nine
in 1945, focuses
on the young girl dying
in the boat to
Ninoshimo Island.

On the man flapping wildly
in circles,

a massive chunk of wood
in one eye. On people

hurling themselves
into water tanks
to soothe all degrees
of their skins.

She does not soothe
her schoolgirl brain
with a geography lesson:

Japan has eight major islands.

Nor does she mention
the cloud
become a cliche

for violence
with breathtaking style.

She quotes the dying girl's
last words:

Tell my mother where I am.

She calls her city
after the Flash
"ocean of fire."

---

*White Flash, Black Rain, ed. and trans. Lequita Vance-Watkins and
Aratani Mariko, Milkweed Editions, 1995.

Afternoon at Fort Washington

The river swells the banks
with each passing boat.
The low-lying trees
opposite
might be moving slightly
as this tiny
orange butterfly,
but they seem so far away,
to be almost stone.

A white sail.
A pebble
in a young boy's hand,
his red shirt on brown skin
in perfect contrast
to the lime-green dress
of the grass.
The boy leans back and throws.

How do I lay down my life
for this child I've never met?
The merest
whiff of infinity
blows through, bracing
as the river's current.

At the Frost Place, August 1984

I am reading Dreiser
in a white motel.
On the table beside the bed
sprigs of goldenrod

clumped in a Mason jar
leave a fine yellow dust.
My skin is covered
with black-fly bites.

The digital clock blinks red.
A coydog howls.
A shotgun fires. A nerve
flickers down the stairs,

igniting in the hallway
the empty
wicker baby carriage.
I do not think of my sons.

Richard Burton has died.
The wind from the east
whistles against the house.
I draw up my knees beneath

the starburst quilt.
The beams creak and give.
They make a lovely sailing sound.
A sort of requiem.

The Arrival of Grace

That is not my daughter
pulled under by a wave.
That is not my daughter
touched all over
by thumbs of salt.

Into her mouth the sea
comes big and hard.
Her lungs give out
a fish music.
It draws the sharks.

The sharks hook
into her lost body.
They flail her skimpy
buttocks black and blue,
cut her in two
in red water
(she will never
bleed like a woman).
This is no magician's daughter.
Pilot fish
    suck her baby nipples.
Pick her tiny clit.

The cow's skull of her pelvis
washes up on the beach.
A dog sniffs it.
Nothing else is given up
to read
    or bury
        or worship.

This was a child of six summers
with a serious daring.

I want to turn the sharks
inside out.

I want to see the moon's agenda
that made that lethal wave
so perfect in its coordinates.
I want to hold the mother
burning up the sea.

Suor Anna

She peers down at the window box
of pink impatiens
outside the iron railing
she clings to for support.
Her jaws toil
as if chewing still
her breakfast
of hard white roll
smeared with jam. She chews
and waits on the balcony
then like a brazen cat
reaches down
to pluck and pluck
a weed from the window box,
the blood rushing to her head
as she stoops,
straightens victorious,
the culprit
dangling from her hand
like a dead mouse.

The French children
in expensive cotton playclothes
race around the tables
in the courtyard.
Suor Anna slowly descends
the stone staircase,
totters without a goal.
Prayers are over.
It is too soon to eat again.

She stops to be greeted
by guests at the convent
who now she is helplessly old
give her kisses
they think she deserves
for cutting off her hair
and living without men.

She receives each admirer,
stranger or friend,
equally, with caution,
as if she'd been given
one of those candies from Murano
made of twisted glass.
She's mistaken them so often
for the real thing.

Teresa's Last Foundation

All of it is here.
—Julian of Norwich

She follows broken twigs,
matted grasses, outward signs
that point to an altar

dim with gold in a town
cut in two by a river.
She will leave in Burgos,

the last of the Carmels,
a veil, a letter,
an alpargata—her shoe

made of rope and canvas.
Like an aging ballerina,
she leaps with less force,

but there is the skill.
She must rest, chooses
a red wooden bench—

with tassels!—to sit on.
All of it is here: the white
pullet at her feet,

pecking for grain. Green
flames of poplars
soaring like steeples.

The mule with velvet eyes
who will carry her to die
in Alba de Tormes.

II

A tear rolls back into its eye.
—Paul Celan, *The Hours and Other Poems*

Madeline Is Melancholy

The sky is rare today
and cruel, tossing back
my black balloons,

pulling from its sleeve
rabbits of cloud.
Dawn laughs, a carping

mother. I sink into a ship
on the ocean floor,
swim through velvet

staterooms with stopped
marble clocks.
Dark-eyed swords

pierce a heart
addicted to remorse.
I'm stuck

with breath, playing
dead to be safe,
my hunger to be sad

a plutonium force
outwitting
the promise of the pearl.

Alias Irene

She broke loose from her father's hand,
turned and found the small cars
circling in their route. Little boys
and girls like her were ringing the bells
of fire engines, tooting horns. No way out.
She pressed against the legs of mothers
and fathers, bumped into lines of kids
all pushing to be first. Maybe someone
here at the carnival could guess her weight
and take her to a place quiet as a church,
where dishes didn't break. Maybe
she could win a kewpie doll with glitter
on its eyelids. Or find a nickel
in the dirt. The woman who found her
that night didn't take her home
but gave her up over the microphone—
"We have a little lost girl called Irene."
Even changing her name didn't work.
She was claimed like a coat, scolded
for disobeying the rule of staying put.
Her father with his lower lip stuck out
held her hand so tight it hurt. Her mother
had that look she got scrubbing the floor
until it shone like a dinner plate.

Bide a Wee

With a touch of the poet,
he named the cottage
Bide a Wee, Scottish
for stay a while.

A summer place
to escape Chicago heat.
To fish. To swim.

There was a small beach.
Once a year they dredged
the lake.
You could wade out
only so far
before your feet touched
cold slime. It would
give and give.

John Murawski died
before I was born,
lost everything in '29
but Bide a Wee,
said to be paid for
with profits
from bootleg gin.

Like so many immigrant
fathers of his generation,
he drank,
he beat his children.

It's his blood
whispering in my veins,
whispering from the lake
overrun with weeds,
tempting me
to break what is fragile.

Old Woman's Pivot Story

When they pulled him from the Grand half-
drowned, we thought he was safe.
He ate boiled cabbage and potatoes.
He worked in the barn.

But the river broke my brother's heart.
Only a week later, he fell in the kitchen.
His hands clawed my arms.
We couldn't find Ma. This time,

my sister Martha and I watched Joe drown.
My feet walked out
on this ledge. For weeks
I could not wash the grave-dirt

from my clothes. And I wonder, still,
why his cheeks were pink in the coffin,
if he woke up in the dark,
what he thought.

Daughter with Camera

There used to be chickens scratching
in the dirt and rabbits out back
in pens too high for me to reach.

The story goes my father was drunk
when he chased my mother with a knife
down this block.

Another time he pushed her, pregnant
with me, and feisty Aunt Estelle
stopped him with a shout.

He's dead now. There's not enough light.
I'm sure the picture won't come out.
I don't tell her that. I slide in

beside her on the seat. She clicks
her teeth, digs for gum in her purse.
Removing the foil, she announces:

"Now you'll always have it. The house."

Blessings and Curses

There's something maternal, even wifely,
in her face—a patience
as she leans into a space she does not deserve.
She's tilting her head toward her father
in front of Sacred Heart church.
She's only twenty, but she looks older.
It's the day of cousin Vernon's first Mass.

Hats were in fashion then. Hers,
a white broad-brimmed sailor, shades
her face round with baby fat. Her flat
chest hides beneath a jacket
stylishly boxy or sizes too big.
Whom is she protecting?

Her father's suit coat strains
at the belly, the thick wavy hair
he's vain about totally white.
He's wearing a tie she gave him,
splashes of blue and red and silver,
the flash of the male.

An ordination is like a wedding—
people give money and cry happy tears.
She won't marry for another five years.
And there will be three children,
a church annulment, a civil divorce.

Before the marriage ends, her husband will
tell her what her problem is.
He will tell her in the kitchen
while she's not watching the rice.
He will jab his finger in the air
and sputter his charged one-liner
with a long half-life:
"Your father ruined you!"

She hears it again tonight,
waiting for the valerian to kick in,
the herb, the label says,
the ancients used to induce sleep.

Did Cassius take valerian?
How different is a natural sleep
from a natural death?

It's been thirty years,
and she can still see her father's dark blood
filling the gallon glass jug
beside the hospital bed.

She wonders now
if, when she stood there,
she did it again—leaned toward him
as she did in the picture,
because she'd grown that way,
like a tree.

What happens to a tree
that takes such a turn
the leaves forget?

If lightning strikes it,
does the burnt split trunk
remember?

Time Piece

She took all the watches she possessed,
including the Bulova, once her mother's, its hands
blue-black as feathers on a Bantam cock.

She was humming, as she dropped them in
the sink, the Eroica theme, the window
steaming the mirror above the suds. Chest

muscles tight, harboring fear. (She's had trouble
exercising on the floor, lying with her
arms spread out like a crucifix,

trying to touch down sideways left and right
her drawn up knees—the pectorals, it seems,
fit to burst.) Time bubbled,

and she sang like the sea, caught in the circle
of fake marble washstand. Sang, scrubbing
the watches, in total sympathy with breakers,

exploding strings of Steinways. And held
her mother's Bulova to her ear, giving
a sad smile to the rest—some floating

on the dingy water, some sinking to the bottom
like wrecks. She thought of blue grooves
in the snow and crossed herself. Rinsed

and rinsed the yellow gold and white, the tin.
Then lined the dripping watches up to dry
on the dresser top. She was listening

for her bliss, right hand on her chest,
in total allegiance. She could hear snow melting
on the mountain range called Blood of Christ.

Law

I grow small.
Against the heavens' yardstick
I have no hands.

Now I am smaller than
the chair,
no more than a mouse
beginning to fear
the dense quiet.

I am eaten by the cat.

I am the purr.

I disappear
through the eye of a needle:
holding the earth together
by an invisible thread.

The Letter

Beyond a child's ken:
urban restrictions
on pets, landlords
nixing kids, paydays
blown by alcohol's
short fuse. In her kitchen
fragrant with baking bread
aunt persuaded me my cat
would never make it
in city traffic.
"Let her stay here
on the farm."

I could respect
the argument for safety.
Didn't fight to keep her,
for the last time spoke
gibberish of cat
into her exquisite ear.

It could be a mercy
the shock of first hearing
escapes me. The letter

three months later.
Learning how she died
nowhere near a car—
a cow crushed her
in the barn—did I cry

or float an inch or two
above my body,
wishing her back,
scratching halfway

up the Christmas tree
as she had that winter,
invisible, shaking
ornaments and tinsel
so hard my aunt,
a believer in ghosts,
crossed herself.

Troubled by an Angel

It was not the cow's fault.
Intent on nuzzling water
from her cup
she stopped, looked up
and saw a spider drop,
never saw the cat slip
into her stall.
But felt its bones break
when she lowered her weight
to the straw. Sometimes
when she can't sleep,
the help cries dying
in the cat's throat
come back like a mother's
dream of a lost child.
It is a familiar place
for hope to die
and the cow's pain is enough
to strip the bark off
every tree she's leaned
on since. For it's then
she meets again the curse
she placed on herself
when, barely a heifer,
she searched the clover-
starred field and could not
find the rich black coat
splashed with white
that warmed her mother.
Oh then, not even the farmer's
fiddle matters, or the perfect
pitch of a salt lick
she smoothed herself.

And when she looks out the barn
it's as if the moon and stars
were falling, and she
is always in the way.

School Physical

He must have a right,
this saint who gave my father
second life, rescued him
from the yellow jaws
of cirrhosis.

Eyes down,
I'm inside the stethoscope,
my knee jerks
for his rubber hammer.
Handsome Italian doctor.

I button my blouse.
He ticks off boxes
on a green form.
I pay him four dollars.
Shame nibbles my smile

as he jokes with me.
I tell no one but the priest
who's in a hurry
and charges the usual
three Hail Mary's.

Home, who'd believe?
He's cut with such success
into my family's marked flesh,
just to say his name
evokes Christ or Roosevelt.

It happens two more times,
this cupping of green breast
as if it were an Easter chick.
Three raids.
A trance of stethoscopes.

A hammer to the ceiling.
I forget about it
until this year of boulders
coming loose in heavy rain.
He's dead. I'm middle aged.

I can change nothing
of the failed landscape
but how I see it. Field
of poppies out of focus.
Jarring trees.

Bride Doll

No "crier"
lived inside
her hollow self

to mime a baby's
voice, but her eyes
worked, could end

the world
with a click. Tall
and thin, moonlight

in her white satin gown,
she was made
of hard stuff,

composition, said to be
a mix of glue
and wood chips. I quickly

tired of her, unfit
for playing school
or house, too focused

on the aisle,
the never-ending
waltz. She could not

sit down. I'm sure
I didn't give her away.
She just disappeared,

may have ended up
in the city dump
choking on her veil

or under a bell jar,
dust-free, antique,
noli me tangere,

loved for nothing
but her style, bewitched
by the dollmaker.

Ignominy on Garland Avenue

*Why do your boys
turn on you?* My mother sips,

moves a spoon, a cup:
a general sticking pins

on a map. I cannot read
her tone of voice. Sad?

Concerned? Triumphant?
Maybe someone said

in anger once,
I hope your *daughter breaks*

your heart. So she must always
strike first, land

her verbal bayonets
and twist. *Wild stallions.*

That's what my husband
calls our three small sons

who disobey. All boy.
I am a silent movie

folding laundry. The sun
in Apollonian irony

is the happy yellow
of Van Gogh's bed. I hug

a stack of blue jeans
to my chest. The floor

floats. The question
never sleeps,

snaps in my head
like sheets on a line.

Petition to a Grandmother

I picture numbers strung
across your chest,
a mug shot. Tell me

what you
or someone else you knew
did to her, the girl

surrounded
by first communion photographs
in cardboard frames

flimsy
as the will
never to sin again. Consider

the cost: the shrug
at intimacy,
focus narrowed

to a needle's eye.
I have no memory
of your daughter holding me.

Mother and Daughter

Smacking her lips,
she cleans her plate
and asks for more.
As if she were still poor.

It's hard for me to look.
I want my mother to be a swan
who never leaves the water,
not this crone
with gravy on her chin.

Aging, why couldn't her passion
have been jewelry?
Or collecting porcelain
angels with violins?

She spreads butter
on her slice of bread.
Bows her head
to the task at hand
like a gleaner at twilight,
too busy gathering bits of grain
to hear the Angelus.

Sutra

The baby, intact, keeps turning up
like a mirage.

Birds stutter. Statues
look back
with eyes demanding life
to stop here.
Something green is hidden,
stripped of expectation
and desire. Variation
on the inside of a drum.
Midnight.

When the heart gives up
on the heart
and the heron of dreams
stalks the river path.
A trickle of sand.
The hexagram.

To understand fawn and maiden
on the forest floor. To bear
the patience of trees,
the panting of animals. Material

witness.
The roof in white code
totally foreign
to what has disappeared:

>   The caress.
>   The blow.
>   The betraying voices.

Packet of ashes.
Wallpaper dark as hearses.

Hand mirror
of imitation horn
face down on the runner
edged with crochet.

Committed Here

She touches to her lips
the rubies of concertos.
She lights the way with a scar.
She truly knows
how good it is to breathe.

Let us applaud
the vicinity of her left eyebrow.
In the original bath,
in the darkest recess of the womb
she refused to die.

With perfect pitch,
she sets fire after fire
to a network of veins,
relinquishing all thought.
The cave lights up.

Silence takes center stage
like cut glass eyes
set in bronze.
She rides the waves
serious as an olive tree.

She has an aura of plutonium
ticking out the dawn.
She sings to the edge of the mind.
A dove flies from her mouth
without martyrdom.

III

—You call this   home? It's
in the heart.—What *literature*!

—Marina Tsvetaeva, "Poem of the End"

A Room Like This

I have read how the world as we know it
started with the Pleiades.
I write with lipstick on the mirror:

"The Pleiades are loose! Pray for us!"
Then sit around looking fatuous
and think of your torso

as if it were worthy of Praxiteles.
As if I really loved you.
I try on the pink plastic slipper

some little girl left on the beach,
and, of course, it doesn't fit. I touch
your phantom eyelash and make a wish.

Our lifelines are risky as the Maginot.
When I hold mine to yours, fear
tries the corners of my mouth

like a bit, my smile at auction.
Don't ask what more can happen.
A room like this? I'm superstitious.

Between a Bullet and Its Target

He and I, oh we believe
in the wrinkles of a word.
We smooth them with our lips and tongues.

We never look down from the ledge,
possessive of the time
left to us. We pay attention

as if these tasks were equal
to laying small white stones in a garden
or arranging a bouquet of mums.

We roll on the grass
taking rapid swallows of our bodies
that will always remember.

Our toes in their shoes
struggle to break out of the leather.
We fall to the floor,

our hearts too buoyant to sink,
and we quiver like thin curtains
at open windows. Come

let us be shadows on the wall,
gold stars on a white field.
Picture the dying children.

Against the Wind

You twist and dive in the sheets,
sleek and undulant. An otter. A greased
Channel swimmer. With light,

regret. Hours of silence in the car
driving back from Ocean City.
I don't drop you at a metro stop,

take you to your door. Home,
a second shower to kill the scent
of cheap motel. I stare at the bracelet

bought with you looking on, bored
and impatient. A trigger. I may never
wear it. Years later, I meet

a man who links your name to mine
as if we'd been an item. Why
lie to him about a nonexistent

us? That night on the beach, snaking
your arm around my waist, you asked
my age. "You carry it well," you said.

I thought of women in *National
Geographic*, sure-footed and poised,
balancing, resigned, heavy

jars of water on their heads.
I walked with you to the motel
against the wind. A war inside.

In a Russian Vein

A political prisoner thaws,
coming back to feeling after a first
arrest. My best gifts stand on their toes,

stretch and leap, the better dancer
shaking free to your applause,
honey from a spoon pulling us closer

to where the tide is. The days
we have left to love slide between the bars,
write themselves out from a wordless

solitary. Had you known me when
we both were invincible, convinced
to be the first death passed by,

you might be crying those guilty tears
for me. For me, wear the order
of the second hand, its tiny revolutions.

Lineage

You try to undo
the can't go home again Wolfe thing,
dig up the address in Poznan.

From the tree's bole,
relatives breathe on the glass.
Where is the author,

the frosty cathedral?
Where is the seven-year cycle of change?
Blood on the planet spins

unrecognized.
Now is not the time
to think of grandchildren

in borrowed caps and spectacles
pretending to be
on stage. Well then,

strike the set. Forget your
father's false face
calling on the saints.

Come out of the bog lit by torches.
The bison turns
mid-cave, and every light

en route to the return
surrenders,
picking up the thread.

Shipwreck

My palms sweat
on the open deck.
My spine balks

in its chalk weight.
The tremendous weight of ships
is no guarantee:

they can break in two
like eggshells.
Beneath the waves

lie currents
even sharks avoid.
Currents can drown,

can leave us changed.
My face pressed close
to an empty shirt,

I can taste the salt.
The wreck begins.
Death pulls up on the beach.

Sunday in Vermont

Sunday morning, thirty below,
my feet first to break
the crust of snow,

no signs posted
to explain the locked door
and empty pews

of the one Catholic church
in Johnson. *To whom
shall we go?* I retrace

my steps, stop a man
dusting off his pickup
to ask where Mass is,

but he's clueless, cryptic
as a rustic in Frost.
I order breakfast

in a bar on Main Street,
bite into my eggs
feeling lost

as one of those babies
left to wail on a church
doorstep, arms

like little apostrophes
beating the air
as if it were the mother.

Snakes at Fort Washington

The snakes have come out early.
It's too hot for mid-May.
We're warned away
from the river path,
but we still take it.
When we don't see a single snake,
I'm almost disappointed.

At the top of the path
where we can lean out
a hundred feet above the water,
I ask for a kiss.
The stiff chrysanthemum
tip of your tongue
darts in my mouth.
It excites me with possibilities

you don't follow up on.
It's as if it were winter
and you'd fallen asleep
in your old skin
while I lie here
coiled and twitching
on the warm rocks.

To Your Good Address

You tell me my sins
in two languages
and speak of my replacement:

>　　the woman with the sad mouth,
>　　the woman who loves children.

Too many times for comfort

you wish me well
in letters, declare
the bleeding hangnail

of your love. Stuck
in your own storm's eye,

you bring high winds.
How can I stop your two-
dimensional hands from

riffling my blouse?
I send you ravens,
quicksand,
a flood on which

to float
your black tongue,
your Panama hat,
your plush tuxedo.

Buttons

She took to using ever stronger
thread, some for winter coats
tough as fishline. It was as if
he were testing her patience
with everything he touched, wrenching
circles of bone, plastic, or wood
through holes, his fingers fierce,
ready to make a fist over her awkward
stitches. She would lower her lids,
poke the thread through the button's
eyes. *Why can't you sew?* he'd whine
when she'd forget. He had watched
his mother align patterns, pin paper
to cotton and wool. Who was this wife
resisting the mold? How could she
presume he would walk the world
with frayed threads, a connection
missing. He expected her to listen,
to be watchful as a wise virgin
for even the threat of a lost mooring.
She continued to forget. She would press
her face against the window glass.
He didn't notice, preoccupied
with the shade he threw
over her bowed head, over the table
with its mound of dark clothing
waiting for her hand to anchor
what he'd torn loose again.

The Audience

The divorce is young, has barely cut
its first tooth. He stands beside her bed,
cap in hand, supplicant, uneasy satellite
circling the wrong planet.

"Then die!" he told her once, angry with her
off the wagon. Now she's doing it,
a yellow-skinned stick figure
burning up the sheets.

Where is the beauty he married? Above
soft aquarium noises—oxygen
bubbling through tubing—he whispers:
"I love you." The strawberry hairs

on his wrist gleam as he pours it
in her ear like a poison. Hearing,
she jerks her head. Her mouth
gropes for a no. Too weak for lies

she signals "go" with a flutter
of long bony fingers. Perplexed,
defeated, he exits, she dies. Later,
he will tell this story with a tease

of bewilderment, clutching a cache
of good intentions to his breast,
letting it spill down the front
of his shirt like a cheap, garish tie.

The Rehearsal

The tree she chose the apartment for is bare.
It's not just the time of year.
Nobody is safe from the trumpets of Sibelius.

When she holds out her hands,
the priest in her trembles.

What does she want with pietas, stark
Spanish madonnas,
their haloes sharp as swords?
The sincere dark settles on her shoulders.

The air is final, cruel
as a stilled bell.
From somewhere higher than the roof

a small white mirror points its finger.

Dark Circle

You are ready again
to carry me clear across the border.
I forget the name of the state
famous for peaches.
I forget my zip code.

Spent, beside you,
I grope my way up
from the same dark
circle in hell
you say we're assigned to.

I am like the Assateague pony
thrusting its head through
an open car window,

longing to be petted,
begging to be fed
a forbidden sweet.

I kiss your eyelids.
There is a black feather
bone-deep in my hand.
I tremble for my joy.

Historic Marker

One drink goes to my head.
At least Iglesias
sings in Spanish for once.
Sunlight falls over your shoulder,
and I think of salt.
The nerve in your jaw works.
The tension spot in my shoulder
tightens in empathy. Packing,
you don't bother to sort.
Cherished or not,
everything's flung in a box.
I go for a walk, hoping
you'll be gone before
I weaken. My steps bring up
holding you in whiskey light,
losing sight of land and history.
It's a day of record-breaking
cold for June in Washington.

Brief

The strange moon shines,
making me a werewolf
before I can count one.
The last veil tears.

The closet I was locked in
shrinks
to the size of a jewel
box, a womb.
Then it's small
as a spot of dust
on a pool, invisible
in moonlight.

The minutes seem charged
with my seeing
the immediate
danger: the intensity
of roses, the cane
breaking my fingers.

I could be killed for
filling out my body.

The surface of my mind
is alive
with petals I have pulled
to prove I am loved.

The silver bullet is you.

The Confession

"I have committed love," the woman says.
"For that," the priest replies, "I gave Degas
a hundred rosaries!" Then, with a guess,

he condemns: "The way you look at him in bed!
No man deserves such worshiping!"
Behind his eyes he sees backstage with Degas

ballerinas adjusting their straps, poised
for the overture. Says, "Do not come down
from your cross. Stones will be bread

soon enough." The tiny grille slides
shut. She lifts the heavy velvet curtain
to face an empty church. Then kneels,

connected once again to the wheat, suffering
her familiar. Who can change the holding
pattern in her knees, her throat's

long memory? Christ's robe of red
stained glass spills rays of carmine light
on her shoulders. A grief at bay

knocks at the gate. She turns to meet
the flood. She is a bubble riding a wave.
Pollen on a bee's wing. She begins to ask

"What is this?" and the words are a gong
vibrating the first sound, penetrating
further and deeper than any angel's dart.

The sun beneath her heart has always known
what her body knows. And then she does
what she does. Equal to the sparrow. Inviolate.

On Reading a Chinese Poet

I see you sleeping
with your wife.
I see you hoarding the eyes
of carp.
I chew on your words
with sensitive teeth.
I swallow the pale
blue sky of the carpet.
You have climbed mountains here.

Meanwhile the furnace creaks
and taps like rain.
The adobe house listens
and waits.

The white irises stir
to the gentlest of mountain breezes
as I slip from my clothes
and douse the light.
All night I shall swim in your river.

I smile at you

like a child
who has just learned to

tie her shoe
or stay inside the lines.

The light changes.
Your jet hair shines above
your black turtleneck.
The water comes without ice,

and I tell you about
Michael on the East Coast
whose finest poems strut
with street talk.

We say goodbye
on the street. The white-
washed walls of the restaurant
are dappled with goldenrod.

Your embrace is chaste,
a friend's. My hands fit
the curve of your back.
My thoughts are intemperate.

A blessing falls
on Cerrillos Road
like warm spattering rain
after a drought.

As the Crow Flies

We drive slow.
A beat-up VW bug slants
empty on the shoulder.
A boy in blue jeans
hugs the road like a bed.
Long hair like my son's.

Only woods and blue
telephone poles
bear witness. Pushed
or fell? An owl
would be a sign.
A crow.

Static burrs
the CB radio.
A woman's voice whines
to steer clear of this
intersection.
Heart of asphalt.
Heart of stone.
Heart of had it coming to him.

We rubberneck
and leave the motionless.

Our goal
Altoona by nightfall,
my partner shifts
to high gear.

For miles
I'm back there,
floating
like Ophelia's hair
on the way things are.

IV

I can't go on. I will go on.
—Samuel Beckett, *Waiting for Godot*

Prologue

I am walking this tightrope.
I am testing the wine.

No stones here. Not even
letters written on sand.
I go into his name

like a heart that knows
its way in the dark.

I would die to see his face.

I am more
than the hungry
magpie scratching on the roof.
I am more than a wildflower.

Chanel's not good enough.
I can't stop kissing his feet.

I break the arms off the crucifix.
I wrap those arms around me
as far as they will go.

She looks everywhere

for the pregnant bride
    who cried in the cathedral.
        She must touch her

working-class hand, tell her
    the jury is out,
        and it's too late

to cop a plea—she will
    probably get life.
        She turns on the radio

for the latest flash from Waco.
    A noise at the door is
        only the wind, the dog

arfs. Beside the porch,
    purple crocuses
        survive late snow

to die. She lingers over
    their petals as if she's lost
        not only the child

with a red ball
    but all memory of its face.
        She wraps this loss

in blue tissue you store
    wedding dresses in.
        Click goes the rebel screen

door. Click go the dog's nails
    on Solarian. Click,
        the retractable ballpoint

pen, the light switch, the unfinished
Schubert lied on FM. The island
with perfect waves.

H.D. Yearning for D.H.

I lie on this
wine-colored blanket,
imagine you

waking beside me
in a pure stillness,
sunlight gilding the birches.

This is my body,
young enough, ready
to claim again

our cliffs of chalk.
My memory of you
(what have I done

with your letters?)
is like a stone
worn silken.

I cast it upon
the waters,
hoping, the devil's

wish granted,
it will change
into bread.

On a Seventh-Century Couple
of Painted Clay

Shall we rest our elbows on four cushions?
Shall you lose your head and one hand,
I only my head?
Shall my nipples show through
my painted bodice
while my ankles turn in a half-lotus?

Shall we discuss dinner then
with our mouths gone?
Shall I attempt nevertheless
to rest my hand on your forehead?
Shall you remember only what your left
hand is doing?

The right stump aches for the softness
of my skin. My skin is a pale blue.

Shall our remaining palms be eloquent?
Shall my belly be flat?
Shall your slim waist be belted
with jewels matching mine winding
like a necklace separating my breasts?

Shall we merely dream of being intact?
Shall we suffer, leaving nothing
to the imagination?
Shall these cushions persevere?

Shall we persevere, this couple of painted clay?
Shall we mutter in our sleep when again
we have speech?
Shall we barely reach forever
in our elegant way?

Shall we find someday we like this better,
not looking at each other,
wearing identical bracelets?
Shall my nipples shrivel?
Shall someone younger smash the portion
that remains?

Shall we stand outside all this play of etiquette?
Shall there be surprise at this ability?
Shall we agree without our bodies, without
our cushions?

Shall we gnash at each other?
Shall we rediscover an old beginning?
Shall we opt to go back to clay
and say this never happened?

Shall the memory too be destroyed?
Shall the air between our fingers
join us like petals?
Shall the peace we do not understand,
undo our painted garments?

Only the fringes of my hair remain.
Touch them with your good hand.

Emma Hardy Speaks from the Grave

It was the cook who held me,
dying. Thomas loved me more
in retrospect, dipping

his pen in the well,
resurrecting Cornwall.
On his writing desk,

he kept a calendar
set to March 7, the day
we met, a fetish

galling to Florence,
his second wife. She
must have been in shock

to split him up
like that: his ashes
taken to the Abbey

for the nation to revere,
his heart here with me
in Stinsford churchyard.

I would have vetoed
the cremation.
Each of us, wanting

so much to be first,
failed to see
Thomas loved best

no woman in the flesh
but the daughter
of his mind: *my Tess.*

Saying the Unsaid

Saying the unsaid,
the understood,
myths laid to rest
come writhing
from their nude address,
deception's body rises
from childhood's grave
and makes the present cast
a source of pain.

Can this embrace
that tastes of musk and rain
be real?

What forces tell me
this shall never be,
poor barren queen?

Strange legacy:
to have seen
the apples bruise
in taking simple air.

I said I love, undid
the house of cards.
Killed the dove.

Choices

He's gone
before you thought
to lift your camera—

a young boy kneeling
by the stream
dividing Taos pueblo

drinking from his hands
water rumored
to be tainted,

his shirt in morning
sunlight a feast
of turquoise. In the air

the scent of pinon,
your fear of horses
and the eerie mountain

said to choose
who must leave or stay here.
You pocket odd-shaped stones

from the stream's bed
and carry them east,
wanting to believe

home is New Mexico,
not where you find it,
not where you lose your life.

Elegy for Green Eyes

I walked through Taos
and could not see the mountain.
I doubted everything

I'd ever written. How I envied her—
eulogies from literati, glowing obits
with classy photographs. Soon

they will publish to great acclaim
drafts and fragments sifted
from notebooks, juvenilia.

And, yes, she'd been happily married.
I hear a scratching noise
from the stove. A bird or a mouse.

The cat jumps. Then it hits me,
like a monitor's whack in a Zendo:
I am jealous of a dead woman!

She cannot sleep, eat, drink,
wrinkle her nose at the passing skunk,
water the knee-high corn.

She cannot feel the cat's tongue
rough as sandpaper. Her glass
is broken. She cannot wake up.

With No Thoughts of Loneliness

The wind moans and multiplies
in Russian olive trees.
Lifts and falls,
an ocean coming in
to hug the walls

of snug adobe.
My mother, Elizabeth,
would not have been afraid
of the sound. Could
go to sleep lulled,

comforted.
I lock up for the night,
my shadow by porch light
elongated, tall
as a pine.

I look back at stars
in a sky shorn of clouds,
almost obsidian.
Beyond town
in the burial ground

of St. Dolores,
pickets
fencing in graves
resemble the slats
of cribs

tilting with death
and sinking.
A dog barks. I carry
my mother's ghost
inside the house.

It flickers and shines,
passing through my hands
like moonlight
before it fades
into the olive trees.

The Fault, Dear Brutus

When police pick him up
in pajamas and bare feet,
he warns of thunder

in every windshield on Main Street.
When they take away his hammer,
he chatters about Venus,

Neptune, which planet
looms closest to the earth,
and sobs from his belly

at sight of his mother
summoned to the station.
He doesn't hear her

cover herself
with fish stories, or see her
do a little dance

at the sergeant's desk.
"He's only fifteen,"
she whispers. Her eyes

go dark, a deep black
silk. "My baby...."
"Thunder!" Twisting

free, he scrambles
for his hammer.
"Thunder! Thunder!"

It takes three men
to hold him down,
jab the needle. He sleeps,

one arm raised
to shield his face
as if it were made of glass.

March

In her crystal: worms on fire
for her flesh, the breakdown

of bone. The rise and fall
slows. She knows the voices

of her children. Why
do they whisper like willows

on the farm? Things grow dark.
She cannot see the moonlight

on her pillow. Is this room
hers? A cold sleep robs

her toes. She's like an ice
floe breaking off.

A slight snap,
then silence without oars.

Memorial Photo—Spoleto Cemetery

Silver hair sleeked back
in a knot, lobes and throat
free of ornament,

her eyes are fierce and dark
as an eremite's,
as Christ's

in Byzantine icons,
weighing a soul.
Without Pietro

thirty-two years,
did she rearrange her life
the way cut flowers do—

barely noticed
as they shift in the vase?
I touch the drawer

she'll lie in
undisturbed
for another generation,

mutter a requiescat,
though my faith's weak
as the candle flame

stuttering
in its red glass house.
Light as a thread,

a ladybug lands
on my wrist, crosses
my skin unafraid

her children will burn.

Shenandoah

The ice is thick, may take my weight.
Tempted to walk on it, I don't,
then feel sad for being wise.
There are footprints in hardened snow,
clear dark patches
where boots have scraped windows
on the Shenandoah.

It's beginning to grow dark.
The last sun peers through
boughs of a giant beech.
I think of the chapel
in nearby Holy Cross Abbey
where for years I've gone to sit
or think or pray,
piecing moment into moment.

What I yearn for isn't bread
but something else.
I can almost taste it.

A sparrow perches on a branch.
Suddenly there are many sparrows.

as I grow old

I have come to know when to brush crumbs from his vest
when to tighten the cummerbund

the puppet movement of brother death
in black and white evening suit he takes off

his hat does that jerking bow of the ambassador
s'il vous plait bone on bone clicking

and rocking the faces carved into the wall
mildly looking on not hearing me cry out

as I touch the dark he comes from
rooting for applause

and it is true this chill comes from within
the night dispelled by one candle

fights to take hold wherever the earth begins
and I close my eyes I close my eyes a baby in my arms

the current taking me waking me
from the dream I am naked in Barcelona

Epistle

You enclose nothing you have written.
And sign your name in so slight a hand
it is barely visible.

Is this really the way?
I have chosen a French red table wine.

No reflection on previous lives,
I come to your mountain pass
afraid to say

you are what telescopes are for.
A white stone
that leans on wrought iron.

A gate that is always open.

TITLE INDEX

A
A Declaration 16
Afternoon at Fort Washington 24
Against the Wind 60
Alias Irene 33
A Room Like This 58
as I grow old 95
As the Crow Flies 76
At the Frost Place, August 1984 25

B
Between a Bullet and Its Target 59
Bide a Wee 34
Blessings and Curses 38
Bride Doll 48
Brief 72
Buttons 67

C
Child Wearing a Red Scarf 20
Choices 86
Committed Here 56

D
Dark Circle 70
Daughter with Camera 37

E
Elegy for Green Eyes 87
Emma Hardy Speaks from the Grave 84
Epistle 96

H
H.D. Yearning for D.H. 81
Historic Marker 71

I
Ignominy on Garland Avenue 50
In a Russian Vein 61
I smile at you 75

L
Law 41
Lineage 62

M
Madeline Is Melancholy 32
March 92
Memorial Photo—Spoleto Cemetery 93
Mother and Daughter 53

O
Old Woman's Pivot Story 36
On a Seventh-Century Couple
    of Painted Clay 82
Only the Sky 21
On Reading a Chinese Poet 74

P
Petition to a Grandmother 52
Prologue 78

S

Saying the Unsaid 85
School Physical 46
She looks everywhere 79
Shenandoah 94
Shipwreck 63
Snakes at Fort Washington 65
Sunday in Vermont 64
Suor Anna 28
Sutra 54

T

Teresa's Last Foundation 30
The Arrival of Grace 26
The Audience 68
The Confession 73
The Dollmaker's Daughter 18
The Fault, Dear Brutus 90
The Letter 42
The Rehearsal 69
Time Piece 40
To Your Good Address 66
Troubled by an Angel 44

W

With No Thoughts of Loneliness 88

FIRST LINE INDEX

A
A political prisoner thaws 61

B
Beyond a child's ken 42

F
for the pregnant bride 79

H
He and I, oh we believe 59
He must have a right 46
He's gone 86

I
I am no chip of broken pottery 16
I am reading Dreiser 25
I am walking this tightrope 78
I grow small 41
I have come to know when to
   brush crumbs from his vest 95
"I have committed love," the woman says 73
I have read how the world as we know it 58

I just got tired of it 18
I lie on this 81
In her crystal: worms on fire 92
I picture numbers strung 52
I see you sleeping 74
It was early. Many 21
It was not the cow's fault 44
It was the cook who held me 84
I walked through Taos 87

L
like a child 75

M
My palms sweat 63

N
No "crier" 48

O
One drink goes to my head 71

S
Saying the unsaid 85
Shall we rest our elbows on four cushions? 82
She broke loose from her father's hand 33
She follows broken twigs 30
She peers down at the window box 28
She took all the watches she possessed 40
She took to using ever stronger 67
She touches to her lips 56
Silver hair sleeked back 93
Smacking her lips 53
Sunday morning, thirty below 64

T
That is not my daughter 26
The baby, intact, keeps turning up 54
The divorce is young, has barely cut 68
The ice is thick, may take my weight 94
There's something maternal, even wifely 38

There used to be chickens scratching 37
The river swells the banks 24
The sky is rare today 32
The snakes have come out early 65
The strange moon shines 72
The tree she chose the apartment for is bare 69
The wind moans and multiplies 88

V
Vuillard painted them 20

W
We drive slow 76
When police pick him up 90
When they pulled him from the Grand half- 36
Why do your boys 50
With a touch of the poet 34

Y
You are ready again 70
You enclose nothing you have written 96
You tell me my sins 66
You try to undo 62
You twist and dive in the sheets 60

www.ingramcontent.com/pod-product-compliance
Lightning Source LLC
Chambersburg PA
CBHW011947150426
43193CB00019B/2930